AIR SHOW

ANASTASIA SUEN

illustrated by CECCO MARINIELLO

HENRY HOLT AND COMPANY · NEW YORK

White clouds, blue sky—
Up above . . .

McDONNELL DOUGLAS F-15 EAGLE (1972)

Hawks soar . . .

CURTISS HAWK 75A (1935)

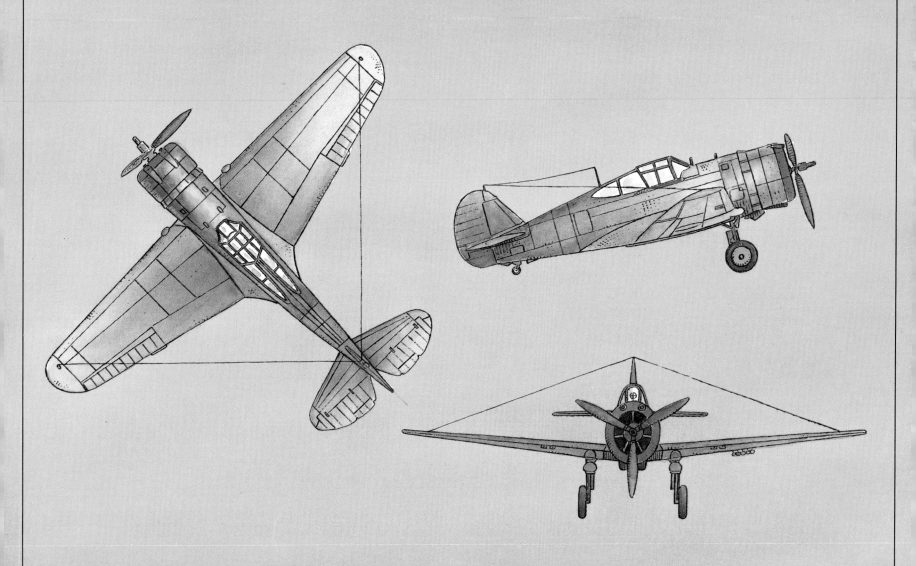

Tigers roar . . .

NORTHROP F-5E TIGER II (1959)

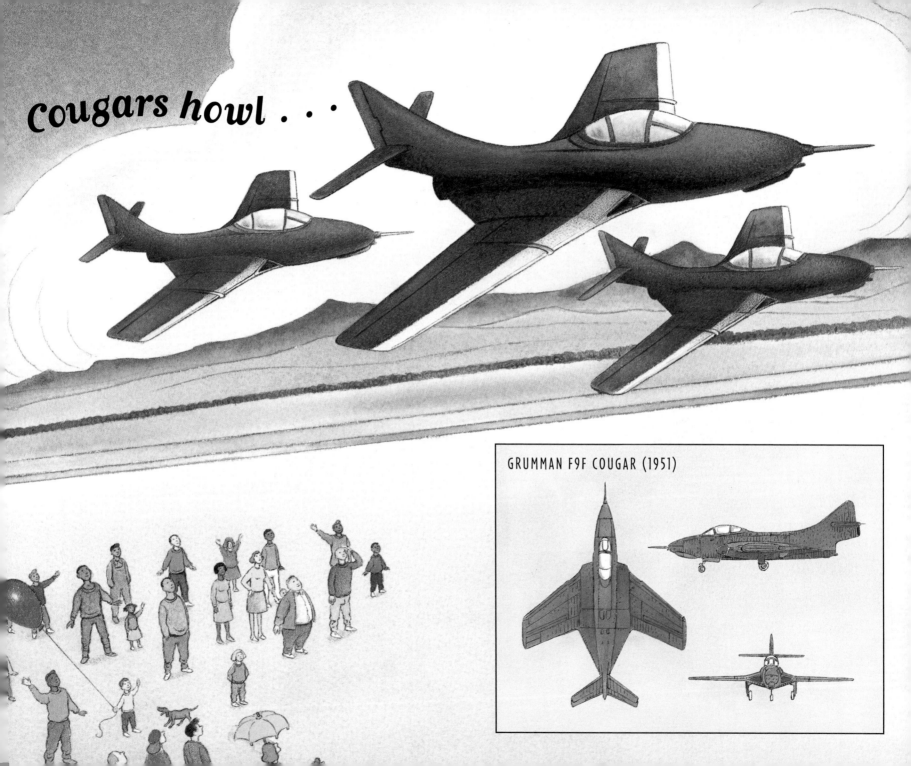

cougars howl . . .

GRUMMAN F9F COUGAR (1951)

Panthers prowl . . .

GRUMMAN F9F PANTHER (1949)

SOPWITH CAMEL (1916)

Mosquitos swoop . . . . .

DE HAVILLAND MOSQUITO (1940)

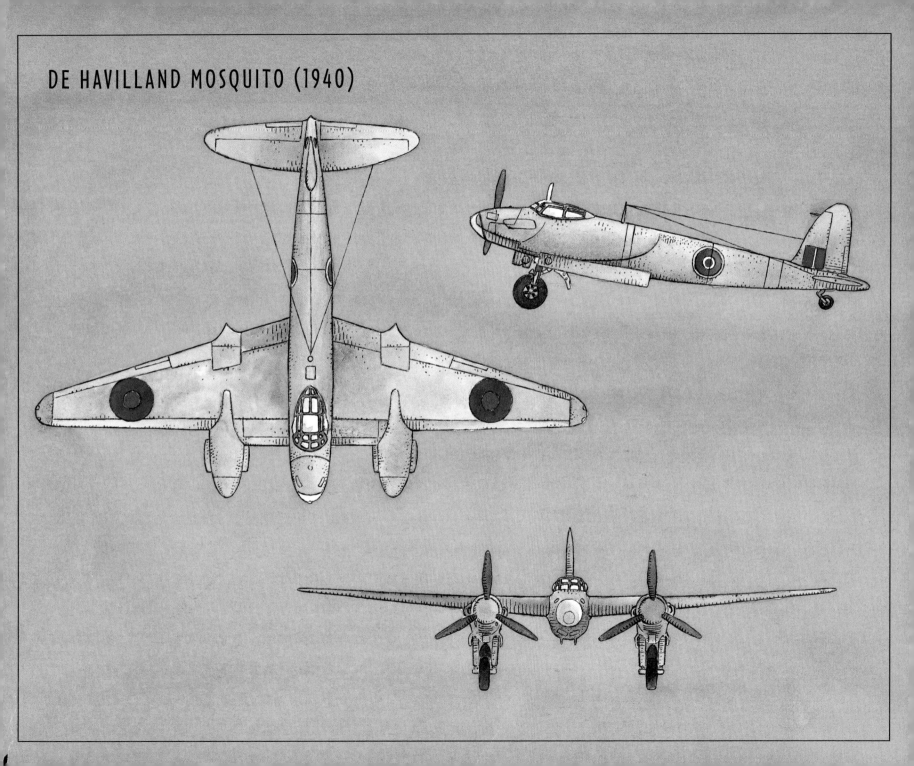

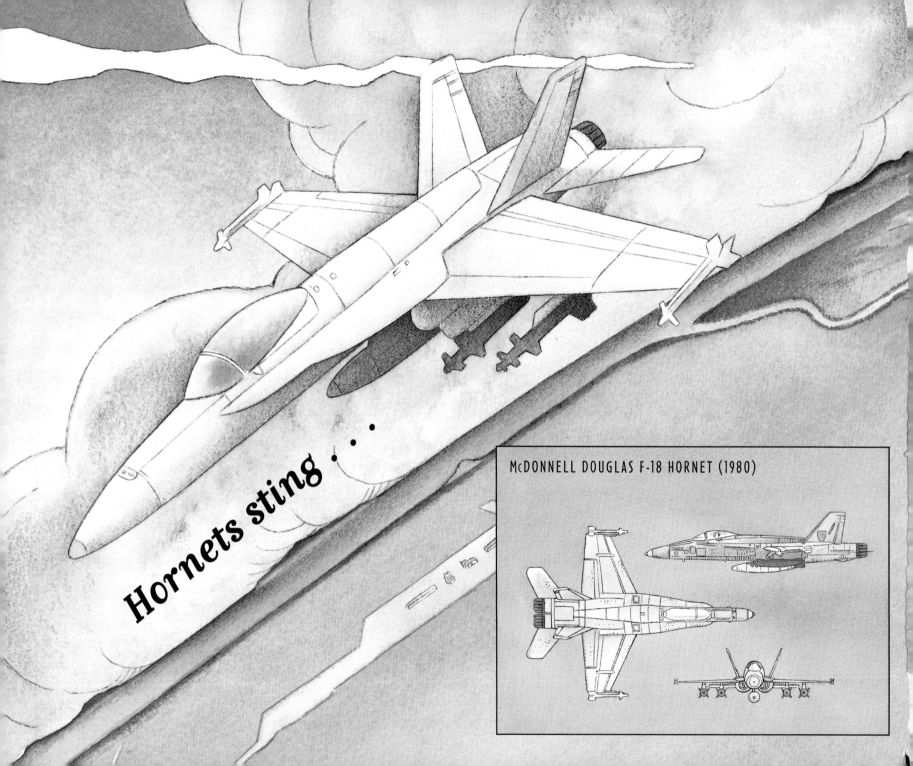

Hornets sting . . .

McDONNELL DOUGLAS F-18 HORNET (1980)

Tomcats sing . . .

GRUMMAN F-14 TOMCAT (1970)

Wildcats creep . . .

GRUMMAN F4F WILDCAT (1937)

Mustangs leap . . .

NORTH AMERICAN P-51 MUSTANG (1940)

Moths flit . . .

DE HAVILLAND 82A TIGER MOTH (1932)

Dragonflies sit.

CESSNA A-37B DRAGONFLY (1967)

Take a look inside—

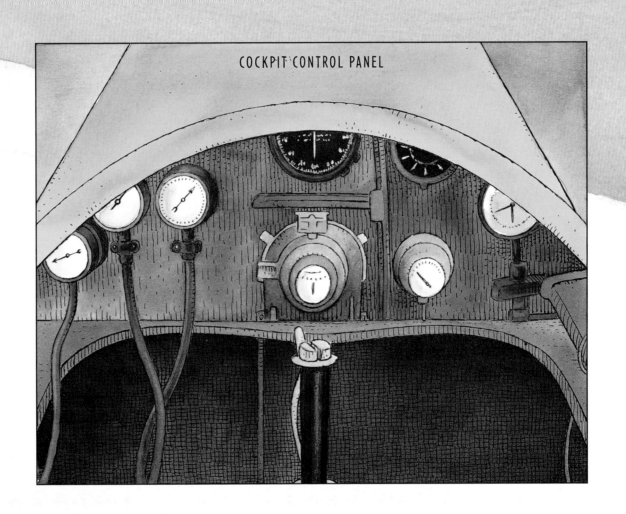

COCKPIT CONTROL PANEL

And come for a ride.

Air Show Stats

SOPWITH CAMEL (1916)
WINGSPAN: 28 FEET
LENGTH: 18 FEET 9 INCHES
HEIGHT: 8 FEET 6 INCHES

DE HAVILLAND MOSQUITO (1940)
WINGSPAN: 54 FEET 2 INCHES
LENGTH: 40 FEET 10 INCHES
HEIGHT: 15 FEET 3 INCHES

DE HAVILLAND 82A TIGER MOTH (1932)
WINGSPAN: 29 FEET 4 INCHES
LENGTH: 23 FEET 11 INCHES
HEIGHT: 8 FEET $9\frac{1}{2}$ INCHES

NORTH AMERICAN P-51 MUSTANG (1940)
WINGSPAN: 37 FEET $\frac{1}{4}$ INCH
LENGTH: 32 FEET 3 INCHES
HEIGHT: 13 FEET 8 INCHES

CURTISS HAWK 75A (1935)
WINGSPAN: 37 FEET 4 INCHES
LENGTH: 28 FEET 6 INCHES
HEIGHT: 8 FEET 5 INCHES

GRUMMAN F9F PANTHER (1949)
WINGSPAN: 38 FEET
LENGTH: 38 FEET 10 INCHES
HEIGHT: 12 FEET 3 INCHES

GRUMMAN F4F WILDCAT (1937)
WINGSPAN: 38 FEET
LENGTH: 29 FEET
HEIGHT: 11 FEET 4 INCHES

GRUMMAN F9F COUGAR (1951)
WINGSPAN: 34 FEET 6 INCHES
LENGTH: 42 FEET 2 INCHES
HEIGHT: 12 FEET $2\frac{1}{2}$ INCHES

NORTHROP F-5E TIGER II (1959)
WINGSPAN: 26 FEET 8 INCHES
LENGTH: 42 FEET 2 INCHES
HEIGHT: 13 FEET 4 INCHES

McDONNELL DOUGLAS F-15 EAGLE (1972)
WINGSPAN: 42 FEET 9¾ INCHES
LENGTH: 63 FEET 9 INCHES
HEIGHT: 18 FEET 5½ INCHES

CESSNA A-37B DRAGONFLY (1967)
WINGSPAN: 35 FEET 10½ INCHES
LENGTH: 28 FEET 3¼ INCHES
HEIGHT: 8 FEET 10½ INCHES

McDONNELL DOUGLAS F-18 HORNET (1980)
WINGSPAN: 37 FEET 6 INCHES
LENGTH: 56 FEET
HEIGHT: 15 FEET 4 INCHES

GRUMMAN F-14 TOMCAT (1970)
WINGSPAN: WINGS EXTENDED, 64 FEET 1½ INCHES
LENGTH: 61 FEET 11⅞ INCHES
HEIGHT: 16 FEET

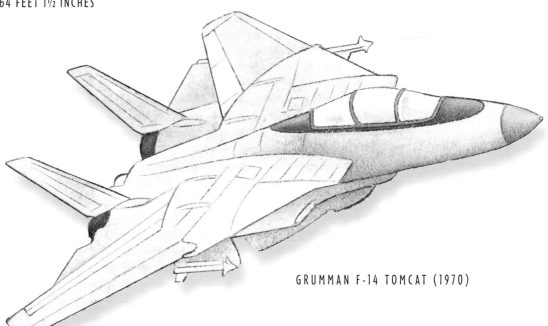

GRUMMAN F-14 TOMCAT (1970)

From a Balloon to the Moon

FAMOUS FIRSTS IN FLIGHT

1783
Montgolfier brothers'
balloon carries two men
into the air.

1849
Sir George Cayley's glider
flies with a ten-year-old boy
as pilot.

1903
Orville Wright flies the
Wright brothers' *Flyer I*—
the first motorized flight.

1906
Gabriel and Charles Voisin
open the first airplane
factory: Voisin Frères
(Voisin Brothers).

1907
Three-man unit established
as the Aeronautical Division
of the Chief Signal Officer
of the U.S. Army.

1907
First helicopter flight: pilot and
designer Paul Cornu.

1908
First flight with a passenger:
Wilbur Wright flies *Flyer III* with
Charles W. Furnas, his mechanic.

1910
First flight from an aircraft
carrier: Eugene Ely flies a
biplane off the deck of the
USS *Birmingham*.

1911
First airmail: six thousand
cards and letters delivered
in Allahabad, India.

1914
First scheduled airliner:
the *Benoist* flying boat
carries passengers across
Tampa Bay.

1924
First flight around the world:
the *Chicago* and *New Orleans*
circle the world in 175 days.

1927
Charles Lindbergh flies alone
nonstop across the Atlantic
in the *Spirit of St. Louis.*

1937
First aircraft with
a pressurized cabin:
Lockheed XC-35, nicknamed
"The Boiler."

1939
First jet aircraft flight:
Heinkel He 178.

1947
First supersonic flight:
Chuck Yeager flies faster than
sound in the Bell X-1.

1952
First jet airliner: De Havilland DH-106
Comet begins commercial service.

1957
First satellite launched into
space: *Sputnik I.*

1961
First person in space:
Yuri Gagarin in *Vostok I.*

1969
First men on the moon:
Neil Armstrong and Buzz Aldrin,
in *Apollo 11* "Eagle."

Air Show was fact-checked by Dom
Pisano and Bob van der Linden, both
experts in the field of aviation.

For Grandpa Daniel and Grandma Lois,
who built the P-51 Mustang —A.C.S.

For Niccolò —C.M.

Cecco Mariniello would like to thank Donato
Spedaliere for his help in researching this book.

Henry Holt and Company, LLC, *Publishers since 1866*
115 West 18th Street, New York, New York 10011

Henry Holt is a registered trademark
of Henry Holt and Company, LLC

Published in Canada by Fitzhenry & Whiteside Ltd.,
195 Allstate Parkway, Markham, Ontario L3R 4T8.

Library of Congress Cataloging-in-Publication Data
Suen, Anastasia.
Air show / Anastasia Suen; illustrated by Cecco Mariniello.
1. Air shows—Juvenile literature. [1. Air shows. 2. Airplanes.] I. Mariniello, Cecco, ill. II. Title.
TL506.A1 S86 2001 629.1—dc21 00-27799

ISBN 0-8050-4952-5
First Edition—2001 / Designed by David Caplan
Printed in the United States of America on acid-free paper. ∞
1 3 5 7 9 10 8 6 4 2
The artist used watercolor on Bristol paper to create the illustrations for this book.